Images of
Maidstone

Images of *Maidstone*

**Kent Messenger
Group Newspapers**

JOHN EVANS

Publishing coordination:
Media House Europe
Sittingbourne, Kent.

The Breedon Books
Publishing Company
Derby

First published in Great Britain by
The Breedon Books Publishing Company Limited
Breedon House, 44 Friar Gate, Derby, DE1 1DA.
1996

Acknowledgements
The preparation of this book has benefited greatly from several
publications edited by the late H.R.Pratt Boorman, proprietor and
editor-in-chief of the *Kent Messenger* for many years. They
include *Hell's Corner* (1940), *Kent – Our Glorious Heritage*
(1950), *Kent Unconquered* (1951), *Kent Inns – a Distillation*
(1955), *Kent Messenger Centenary* (1959), *Pictures of Maidstone*
(1965), *Kent A Royal County* (1966), *Spirit of Kent* (1968) and
Kent Our County (1979). Much help has also been received from
members of the photographic department of the *Kent Messenger*,
who took most of the pictures, Kent Messenger Group Central
Information Unit and former staff journalist Roy Plascott.

ISBN 1 85983 063 3

Printed and bound by Butler & Tanner Ltd., Selwood Printing
Works, Caxton Road, Frome, Somerset.

Colour separations by Colour Services, Wigston, Leicester.

Jackets printed by Lawrence-Allen, Weston-super-Mare, Avon.

Contents

Introduction

by John Evans

THIS is not an attempt to present a detailed history of Maidstone – there are several specialised studies available. Rather it's a pictorial dip into what to some is All Our Yesterdays, to others is All Our Never Was – the years 1930-1970.

The most crucial happening was, of course, World War Two, which brought in its wake a far-reaching social revolution the effects of which have not yet been completely appreciated.

Maidstone was synonymous with firms like Tilling Stevens, Rootes, Foster Clark and Sharps. Farmers called Day, Fermor and Worley had seemingly tended the land since the dawn of time.

Well, how things have changed, or was it ever thus? Did they ever have that permanence that is associated only with youthful memory? These pages will show that few aspects of life remain unamended for long, although without doubt the pace of change was much slower in the period under scrutiny.

It is significant that at this distance, even 1970 can be seen as a vastly-different era. Not just the obvious things like cars, shops and clothes have altered – it's the atmosphere, the very essence of everyday life.

There was a greater sense of order, less crime, more respect for tradition. Words like political correctness and counselling had not been thrust upon a public that surely would have been no more prepared then to accept them than their 1930 forerunners. Feminism had emerged to an important degree during the war, but no one called it that until much later.

At this stage we can appreciate that round about 1970 some of the more significant aspects of the upheaval first took hold. We were to become more questioning, more prepared to thumb noses at what was perceived to be unwarranted authority.

Maidstone, always in the centre of things in Kent, was bound to be influenced by this elimination of the acceptance of the status quo and its replacement by a spirit of protest that rapidly developed into an industry.

Let me give you one example. Our pages reflect the excitement that greeted the construction of what was then called the Maidstone Bypass and is now a vastly extended M20.

In the 1950s and 1960s we were still firmly of the belief that cars were symbols of the better life we had been promised after the war and that we needed good roads on which to enjoy them.

Today cars, like smoking, are regarded as harbingers of mankind's downfall; motorways as destroyers of everything that is essential in the environment. As always, there is little realism about the arguments or the extremes that provoked them.

It was obviously not like that in the 1930s. Britain had not long emerged from the horrors of a devastating war and another, even more overwhelming conflict was only a few years' hence. But there was a formal structure about life, about work and recreation, that was to last until the 1960s began to swing.

Or is it that distance has conveniently created enchantment? In any event, Maidstone was inevitably in the forefront of any new thinking. Despite its long-assumed importance as the County Town of Kent, Maidstone had spawned a permanent sense of rebellion among its people – what we today call sheer bloody-mindedness.

Consider Maidstone's turbulent past. This was where a famous commoner, Wat Tyler, led the Peasants' Revolt in the 14th century and where later defiance against the crown was headed by the grander Sir Thomas Wyatt.

Maidstone, let it not be forgotten, twice lost its Royal Charter because of its refusal to buckle down and do as it was told.

Perhaps it was because of its earlier dominance by the Church that Maidstone played a part in the Civil War that would have today's media beside itself with excitement. It was, after all, Maidstone's Roundhead Mayor, Andrew Broughton, who read out the proclamation of the death sentence on Charles I. Little wonder that he became a subsequent darling of the town's Left.

The Battle of Maidstone, in which the Roundheads drove the King's forces up Gabriels Hill in 1648, was the first major Parliamentary victory.

Yet for so many years the development of the town proceeded along measured lines. It has long returned Conservative MPs to Parliament, for instance.

Its location made it the natural centre of Kent and thus a key influence on its becoming the County Town against the perhaps more obvious 'establishment' claims of cathedral cities Canterbury and Rochester.

There were considerable advantages derived from the River Medway, which allowed Maidstone to transport its goods long before effective road and rail transport was in place.

It is also important to remember that Kent is not known as the Garden of England without just cause, much as many regret today the disappearance of large parts of that garden and the surrender of a once-dominant industry to what appears to be permanent transition, not to say foreign control. Good soil led to successful farming, however, and even today there are few richer agricultural areas.

Maidstone was, and remains, an obvious focal point. It's the home of Kent County Council, which is now the area's biggest single employer and stands defiantly trying to ward off the threat of yet further drastic reorganisation.

Maidstone is the headquarters of a vast number of organisations. It used to be the centre of much progressive and varied industry, notably brewing – oh, the smell of the beer! – papermaking, foodstuffs, motor engineering, cement, quarrying.

By 1970 much of this had either gone or was clearly on the way out. So the town was left to struggle against the economic problems of the late 20th century, not knowing quite where it was going to end up but determined to make the best of things.

Critics will point to redevelopment, especially in the 1950s and 1960s, that has been haphazard and at best, far to everyone's liking. Maidstone was never a pretty town – it was a commercial, working town – but even more than many such places, it lost much of its character with the ceaseless quest for commercial uniformity.

Where once it boasted a delightful array of individual shops and small businesses, now it is mostly chain stores, building societies and malls.

This is almost inevitable, given our demands for so-called convenience and a pace of life that unfortunately permits little in the way of escape from everyday cares. Where Maidstone has to search its soul, nevertheless, is in its lack of a worthy theatre or concert hall, a major hotel even, and its inability to make even a modest impact in the sporting world.

Any major town with a river running through it is bound to suffer traffic problems approaching nightmare proportion. Maidstone's are certainly in the Premier Division for frustration. But increasingly it is making better use of its most obvious natural facility. At last there are signs of responsible riverside development.

The annual river festival, allied to a continuing tradition of town carnival and similar joyous celebration, enhances community activity that remains encouragingly strong in town and village, albeit considerably more boisterous than most of what is pictured in this volume.

Maidstone may be misguided in seeking the benefits that current thinking insists can be derived from 'tourism', which to many is basically alien to the very nature of the place. But there again, Maidstone is showing its determination to succeed.

It may have to compromise, to keep on changing. Which is where we came in, all those years ago.

The heart of Maidstone in the 1950s, dominated by Rootes' factory, with County Hall prominent in the

background and the Maidstone & District bus depot in the foreground.

Maidstone bridge (see also next page) was already constantly jammed with traffic by 1960. One of the first major road

schemes opened up Bishops Way in 1964. The impact on the landscape is clearly shown in the picture taken in 1967.

The top of the High Street in 1967, with the Queen Victoria monument and the Town Hall to the fore. The scene

is dominated by the splendid Westminster Bank building.

In the centre of town on August Bank Holiday Monday 1939, with the outbreak of World War Two only a few days away.

Public conveniences by Maidstone Canon in 1935. The danger to pedestrians from increasing traffic brought about their closure.

Week Street was busy on Easter Saturday 1937.

Maypole, David Greig and Rego – familiar trading names in the Week Street of 1936. Note the absence of street markings.

The summer of 1935 with the *Kent Messenger* preparing for extensive development that saw its printing works established. They were in service for more than 30 years.

Lower Stone Street in 1936.

Mothers seek bargains as T.Button's held a closing down sale in Gabriels Hill in the 1930s. Compare the pram with today's baby carriages.

One of the best-known stores in Maidstone, Chiesmans closed in 1983 after 50 years' service.

The Beehive, at the junction of Week Street and Union Street, was one of those marvellous shops that sold almost everything. Do places like it still exist?

The clothes look drab, but by 1950 Britain was beginning to rid itself of post-war austerity. This was the queue for a sale at Dunnings the drapers in Maidstone that February.

In the following few photographs, Old Maidstonians will recognise some of the shops, almost all of which have long since gone. The pictures were taken during World War Two, as indicated by several clues. This is the lower part of High Street.

Another view of Week Street.

Gabriels Hill, with the Palace cinema on the right.

Lower Stone Street.

Week Street, with its celebrated coffee shop. Note the decorative pargetting plasterwork, a feature of several Maidstone buildings.

Market Buildings.

Upper Stone Street.

Work in progress in Bank Street/Middle Row in 1959. New buildings were to shut off this view thereafter.

The Town Hall in 1936. It was built in 1764 and has remained relatively unchanged.

The Mill Street-High Street junction in 1959.

Another 1959 picture, with the then Haynes Brothers' premises the key feature of the Week Street-King Street-Gabriels Hill-High Street junction.

Horses were still being used to transport railway goods in 1953.

A bad day for business
– Earl Street in 1956.

There were no traffic lights
at the top of the High Street
in 1933. The policeman had
to be especially vigilant.

Maidstone Golf Club in London Road gave way to housing development in the early 1960s.

The 1950s and 1960s saw tremendous building programmes, although not all the dreams of better lifestyles were to come true. Maidstone changed as much as anywhere as the next four pictures show. This one features Shepway Estate nearing completion. *Picture courtesy of FotoFlite, Ashford, Kent TN23 1ES.*

Ringlestone Estate in 1947.

Park Wood in the mid-1960s.

The junction of Sittingbourne Road and Penenden Heath Road in 1959.

Maidstone Market put the town on the county's business map for centuries. It was first held in 1267. This was the scene at the Lockmeadow home of the market on a typical Tuesday in 1950.

A magically relaxed group of Maidstone families enjoying themselves at Penenden Heath in 1956. No other picture could so clearly embrace the social changes of the last 40 years. Ironcally, this was once the site of Maidstone's public hangings.

The County Police Headquarters in Sutton Road in 1958.

Maidstone Prison in 1958. It was originally built in the period 1811-19 for £200,000. *Picture courtesy of Foto Flite, Ashford, Kent TN23 1ES.*

Trolley buses still had years of service left in December 1964 when Bishops Way was opened.

The town's first multi-storey car park opened in Medway Street in 1962.

The Tyrwhitt-Drake Carriage Museum in Mill Street, housed in the 14th-century Archbishops' Stables. This picture was taken in 1954.

Maidstone College in 1967. It was founded in 1395 as the College of Priests.

The Archbishops' Palace originally dates back to 1205. It was rebuilt more than once and became public to mark Queen Victoria's Golden Jubilee in 1887.

Archbishops' Palace, looking across the river in 1960.

Perhaps the best-known of Maidstone's buildings, County Hall was originally opened as the Sessions House in 1915. This picture was taken in 1933.

By 1939 the premises were extended and officially named County Hall, headquarters of the County Council.

Mote House in Mote Park in 1963. For many years it was a Cheshire Home for the physically handicapped.

Brenchley Gardens, a quiet retreat from Maidstone's busy centre, in 1966. St Faith's Church overlooks the gardens.

The County Council library at Springfield was opened in 1964.

High-rise flats appeared in the 1960s – these are at Mote Road.

Maidstone & District Motor Services' depot in Knightrider Street in the 1930s, with an impressive parade of staff and vehicles.

The scene in 1933 as all the Maidstone & District buses were cleaned every night – long before mechanical aids eased the work.

Another long-lost scene. A Maidstone & District ticket collector on duty in 1937.

Knightrider House, the headquarters of Maidstone & District Motor Services, in the 1940s.

Maidstone Corporation ran its own services of buses, trams and trolley-buses for many years from the early 1900s until eventual privatisation in the 1980s. This was one of its smart fleet in 1932.

Originally Fremlins brewery, the Victorian premises in Earl Street were demolished in the early 1980s and became a Whitbread distribution depot. This 120ft chimney was a dominant feature of the Maidstone skyline for many years.

One of the town cinemas that closed in the 1950s and 1960s, The Regal in Faith Street became the Trustee Savings Bank.

The old Sharps sweet factory at Fairmeadow by the Medway, in 1962.

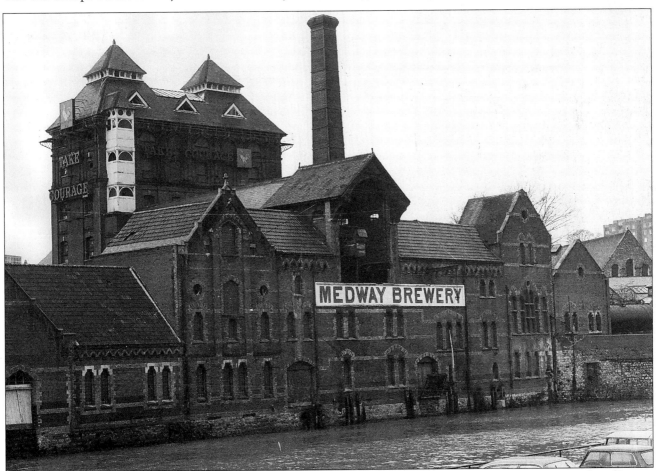

Medway Brewery – originally Style & Winch and then Courage-owned – was another riverside industry whose life ended in the early 1970s.

Tilling Stevens, the coach and commercial vehicle manufacturers, in St Peter's Street in the 1940s. It became part of the Rootes empire in 1950.

Maidstone electricity works in the 1950, part of a heavily-industrialised area at Fairmeadow that occupied much of Maidstone's riverfront.

By the late 1960s there was no longer the chance to try Maidstone-produced Pocock's bread.

Maidstone Fire Brigade members in 1938.

Regimentation was the order of the day for this all-female workforce at Barming Canning factory in 1936.

In 1966 there were still clear distinctions between men's and women's work in many organisations. This was the scene at Kent Fire Brigade headquarters in Maidstone.

The reporters' room at the *Kent Messenger* headquarters in Week Street in the mid-1960s.

Agricultural business under way at Maidstone Corn Exchange.

Imagine this today – sheep being driven to market across Maidstone bridge in 1930.

No animals rights protesters at Maidstone Fair in the 1930s, but a lone policeman was there to maintain order.

Maidstone's importance as a farming area is perfectly illustrated by this 1947 scene just on the outskirts of town.

Harrietsham in September 1956. Mechanisation was having a marked effect on farming.

Ploughing at Aylesford in 1951 did not seem to have changed for many years.

Sheep dipping at Boughton Monchelsea in 1954.

Time for a breather during
harvesting at Hockets Farm,
Detling, in 1971.

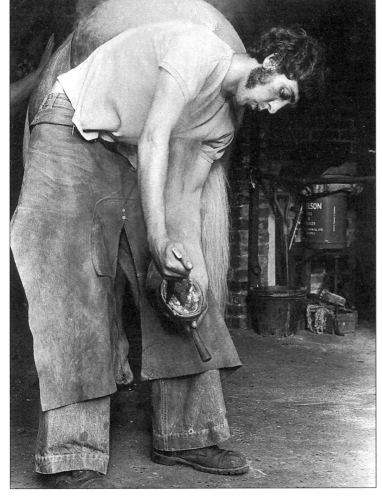

A traditional craft – Trevor
Stern, of Yalding, was the
area's champion blacksmith
in 1970.

The merging of town and country was never better epitomised than at hopping time. For scores of years hop-pickers, many of them from London, descended upon Kent in the autumn for a combination of hard work and holiday. This family scene was captured at Hermitage Farm, Wateringbury, in 1958.

Young and old joined in – this picture was taken at Rugmore Farm, Yalding in 1964.

The old methods were on their way out by 1970, when Mr and Mrs Neville showed the value of teamwork at Clock House Farm, Hunton.

British Red Cross Society members checking on the health of hoppers at Tutsham Hall, East Farleigh, 1950s.

In 1960 the opening of Maidstone by-pass, now the M20, was to have significant effects on the area. This was the scene at the Maidstone-Chatham Road, near the Running Horse, in 1959 as road improvements were carried out in readiness for the motorway.

Ceremonial Maidstone
Royalty, VIPs, Civic Affairs

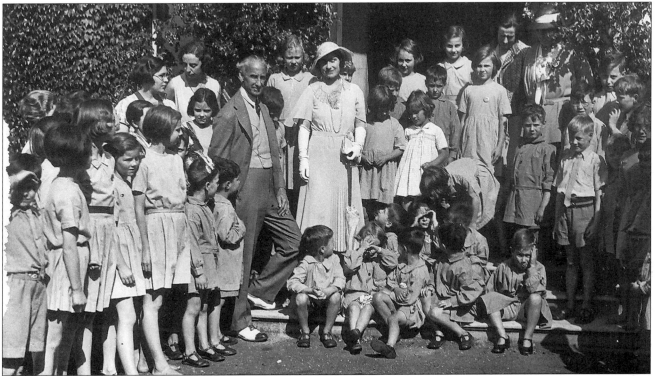

The Duchess of York – later the Queen and then the Queen Mother – visits poor children at the Caldecott Community in Mote House, Maidstone in 1933.

Prince George, the Duke of Kent, chats to an officer of the Girls Life Brigade during a tour of the County Fair at Mote Park in 1935.

The Duchess of Kent, Princess Marina, meets a wounded war veteran at Preston Hall Hospital in 1936.

Maidstone is lit up to celebrate the coronation of King George VI and Queen Elizabeth in 1937.

The Duke of Kent – father of the present Duke does his royal duty and inspects members of Maidstone Auxiliary Fire Service in 1941.

The Duke of Kent, in his role of Inspector of Factories, visited war workers at Tilling Stevens in Maidstone in 1941.

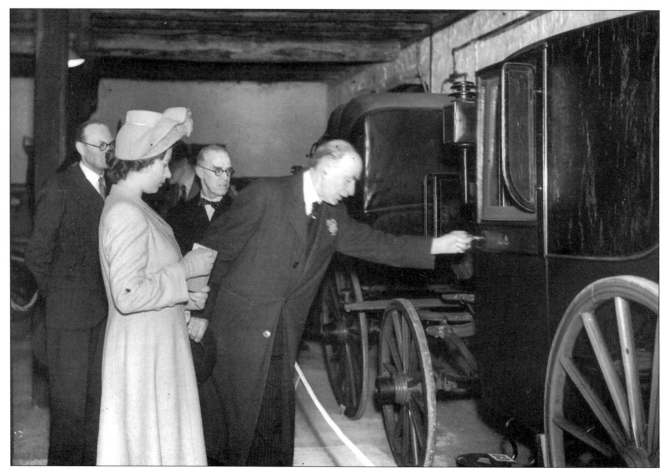

Princess Elizabeth came to Maidstone in November 1946. She was shown round the Carriage Museum by the Mayor, Alderman Sir Garrard Tyrwhitt-Drake.

Princess Elizabeth with the vicar, Canon Standing, at All Saints' Parish church.

Princess Marina visited Maidstone in 1943 to see the work of Civil Defence and other services. Here she is talking to nurses outside County Hall.

The Mayor, Alderman B.J.Watson, heads the civic party at the proclamation ceremony for Queen Elizabeth I

...outside Maidstone Town Hall in February 1952.

Lady Louis Mountbatten met St John Ambulance Brigade nurses at the Ophthalmic Hospital, in 1942.

Princess Alexandra sees rug-making during her visit to the County Show in 1958.

The present Duchess of Kent provides a memorable moment for a youngster in 1967, when she officially opened the 'Y' Centre in Maidstone.

The Duke and Duchess of Kent are welcomed by Lord Cornwallis as they arrive at the County Show in 1968.

Sir Winston Churchill was a guest at the County Show in 1948, when the wartime Prime Minster was Leader of the Opposition.

Prime Minister Sir Anthony Eden visited West Malling Royal Air Force station in 1956 to present a trophy to No 500 (County of Kent) Squadron, Royal Auxiliary Air Force.

The Mayor of Maidstone, Councillor F.G.Shrubsole, presides over a session of the Town Council in 1936.

Maidstone Corporation in procession from church in May 1937.

Maidstone Town Council pose before starting a meeting at the Town Hall in 1960. Councillor Winifred Goodchild

A full meeting of Kent County Council at County Hall in 1962.

was the Mayor.

Members of Maidstone Rural District Council in October 1959. The authority disbanded in the local government reorganisation of the 1970s.

The 1930 Remembrance Day service at the Cenotaph in Brenchley Gardens.

Kent police officers receive medals to mark the Silver Jubilee of King George V in a ceremony at Wrens Cross, Maidstone, in May 1935.

Assize judges leave their lodgings in Lower Stone Street in 1964.

Members of the Queen's Own Royal West Kent Regiment, whose home was in Maidstone for 87 years until amalgamation with The Buffs in 1961, at a reunion in the town in 1936.

The 1st Battalion, Royal West Kents, march down Week Street to mark their return from Malayan service in March 1954.

The Mayor, Councillor F. Leslie Wallis, takes the salute at the Town Hall in August 1956, when Maidstone gave

the Freedom of the Borough to Kent's Royal Air Force Bomber Squadron 500.

People and Events – Disasters, Personalities, Celebrations

Maidstone regularly suffered from severe flooding until improvements were made by the banks of the Medway. One of the worst floods was in 1936.

People waited for lorries to get them through the water at the bottom end of High Street in 1953.

The clothes suggest it was a nice day – apart from the extent of these floods in 1968.

The Central Cinema never reopened after being damaged by fire in the summer of 1955.

One of Maidstone's worst fires caused the deaths of three firemen at Oakwood Hospital in 1957. The tower collapsed on them after the fire had been extinguished.

Men from many fire brigades in the county attended the funeral of the men killed in the Oakwood disaster.

Foster Clark's printing works suffered badly in August 1961.

St Paul's Church was virtually destroyed in 1963. It was rebuilt and opened in more modern form in 1971, the dedication being by the Archbishop of Canterbury.

Traders in Week Street became so exasperated at the time road repairs were taking in 1955 that they used the holes as places to plant trees, flowers and vegetables.

Sir Garrard Tyrwhitt-Drake was one of Maidstone's greatest personalities. He was 12 times Mayor of Maidstone and a dedicated worker for civic and charitable causes. Sir Garrard was knighted in 1936 – three years after this picture was taken of him riding at the head of the town carnival procession.

Sir Garrard with some of the ponies at his zoo park near his home in Cobtree, which he and Lady Tyrwhitt-Drake ran for many years.

Sir Alfred Bossom was Conservative MP for 28 years. This ceremony marked his 21st anniversary as the Member for Maidstone. He was presented with his portrait by Miss Katharine Samson, a long-time worker for Sir Alfred.

Sir Alfred was succeeded by John Wells – later Sir John – who represented Maidstone from 1959 until 1987. This picture dates from the early 1960s when he was making a point in favour of farming interests by riding a horse to Parliament while formally dressed.

Lord and Lady Monckton with their family at Harrietsham. They previously lived in Bearsted. Lady Monckton was to become the first woman to hold the office of High Sheriff of Kent in 1981 and Lord Monckton played a leading part in public life in the county.

Maidstone Alderman Sir Gordon Larking, who achieved distinction as national president of the British Legion – later the Royal British Legion – which has strong connections with the area through its village near Aylesford. This picture is from a Legion ceremony in the early 1970s.

Sir John and Lady Best-Shaw at their Boxley Abbey home in 1971. Sir John, who had a distinguished naval career, was High Sheriff of Kent in 1960-196l and represented Hollingbourne Rural and Boxley Parish Councils for many years.

Sir William Rootes, later Lord Rootes, at the County Show in 1950. He was head of Rootes Ltd, the motor firm of Maidstone, Rochester and Wrotham and had many other interests.

Richard Hearne, the children's entertainer better known as Mr Pastry, lived at Bearsted and was a familiar figure in the Maidstone area for many years. In this picture he is playing the fool during a 1959 visit to the *Kent Messenger*.

Formality was the keynote of pre-war days (and for a good many years afterwards). This was Maidstone Rotary Club in 1931.

One of the most successful organisations for youngsters was the *Kent Messenger* Keg Megs Club, which was launched in 1928 and ran for more than 50 years. Apart from giving members a good time, the Keg Megs raised thousands of pounds for charity, especially hospitals. This was the scene at a 1950s gathering in Maidstone.

The *Kent Messenger* organised a Christmas party for poor children in Maidstone every year from 1891 until 1939 when they were halted because of the threat of bombing after the outbreak of war. This was the incredibly orderly scene at the last party.

For several years in the 1960s the *Kent Messenger* 50-mile Walk from Margate to Maidstone attracted thousands of entries – the forerunner of many such efforts for charity. Fancy dress was already in evidence at this starting point. Note the car park charges.

Youngsters make the most of the big freeze in Mote Park lake during the dreadful winter of 1963.

A timeless scene from members of the Salvation Army in Earl Street. The year was 1965.

Protests became a way of life in the 1960s and 1970s, but this one against the Vietnam War – at the Broadway war memorial in 1968 – looks gentle enough.

A Maidstone
Corporation tram
in the town centre
in 1936.

The tram service later
switched over to trolley buses
before it came to an end in
1967 after a total of 53 years.
After that ordinary motor
buses were used.

Everyone looks very subdued at this party in George Street, Maidstone, to celebrate King George VI's coronation in 1937. Perhaps the Mayor, Alderman J.Hillier French, made too long a speech.

In retrospect, the other great coronation year events, marking Queen Elizabeth II's crowning in 1953, perhaps represented one of the last examples of an age of innocent pleasure, as the following sequence illustrates. Ditton children were presented with Bibles at Cobdown sports ground just as the coronation service started.

Decorations going up at County Hall.

A model of the coronation procession fascinated children at Plains Avenue County Primary School.

Merrie England in Oakwood Park looked back at the first Elizabethan era.

Margaret Law, queen of the celebrations in Weavering, was crowned by Maidstone Mayor, Alderman Thomas Armstrong.

Congratulations to Cadet Derek Booker from Lt Cmdr H.A.Skinner, commanding officer of Maidstone Sea Cadets, on being chosen to represent the unit at the coronation.

Flags fly at Coxheath, brightening what proved to be a disappointingly cold day.

All smiles at the Foster Clark Estate party.

Churches, Hospitals, Schools and Pubs – in town and surrounding villages

The parish church of All Saints', by the River Medway, dates back to the late 14th century. It is one of the largest examples of a perpendicular church in England.

A service in All Saints' in 1963. The nave is 93ft wide.

St Francis' Roman Catholic Church in Week Street in 1963.

By the time this picture was taken in 1970, St Francis' had lost its spire.

The Congregational Church in Week Street is virtually hidden between shops. This was the church in 1964.

Tonbridge Road Methodist Church in 1964.

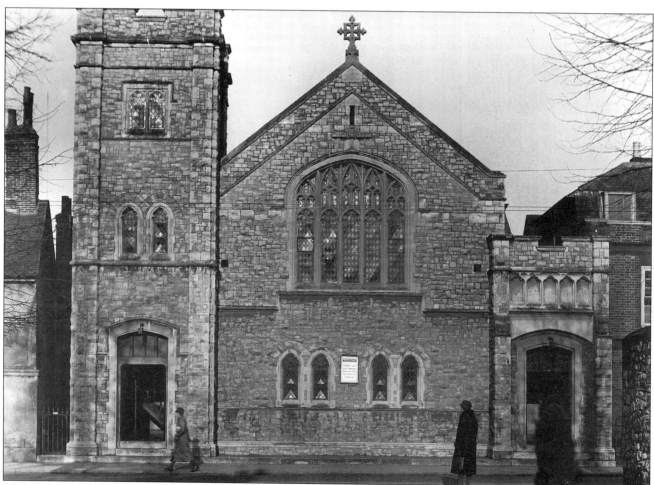

The Baptist Church in Knightrider Street in the 1930s.

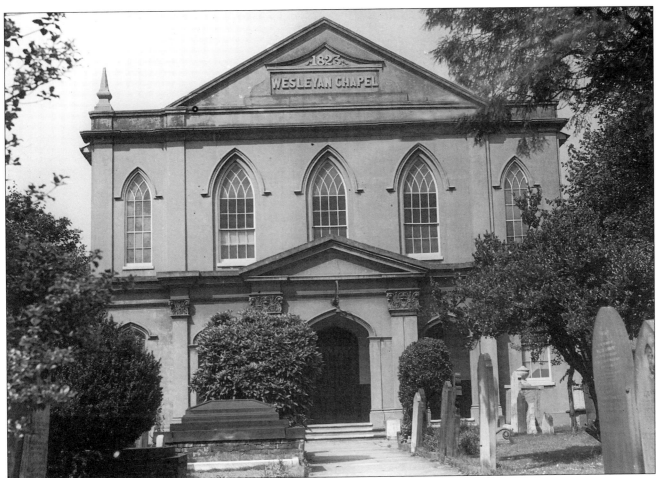

A 1940s picture of the Wesleyan Chapel, off Union Street.

St Peter's Church in 1937. Said to be the oldest building in the town, it was forced to close in the early 1980s.

Another redundant church, Holy Trinity, near the Ophthalmic Hospital. This picture was taken in 1966, some years before the church fell into disuse.

St Stephen's at Tovil appears to be closer to the town centre than it really is.

The Church of St Peter and St Paul at Leybourne, renowned for its unique double heart shrine.

St Margaret's, Barming in 1969.

Waiting for a wedding party to leave St Peter and St Paul's in Teston in 1964.

A civic ceremony at Boughton Monchelsea Church in the summer of 1958.

Thurnham Church
in 1962.

All Saints' at West Farleigh
prepared for harvest festival
in 1966.

The parish
church at
Otham in the
1960s.

All Saints', Ulcombe, in
1965.

Langley Parish
Church in December
1955.

A 1964 picture of
Hollingbourne Parish
Church.

The Church of St Nicholas at Leeds in 1970.

Linton Parish Church in 1963.

Leeds
Parish
Church,
1966.

Bearsted's
Church of
the Holy
Cross in
1964.

St John's Church at Cobtree Hall in 1967.

West Kent Hospital in Marsham Street was in service for more than 150 years before the new Maidstone hospital opened at Barming in the 1980s.

The nearby Ophthalmic Hospital, specialising in the treatment of ear, nose, eye and throat ailments, was established in Church Street in 1847. It was scheduled for relocation in amalgamation proposals in the mid-1990s.

Preston Hall Hospital was the cornerstone of the British Legion Village, where many ex-Servicemen were cared for.

Originally Barming Mental Hospital, later Oakwood Hospital and the Maidstone Hospital Psychiatric unit. This pictur

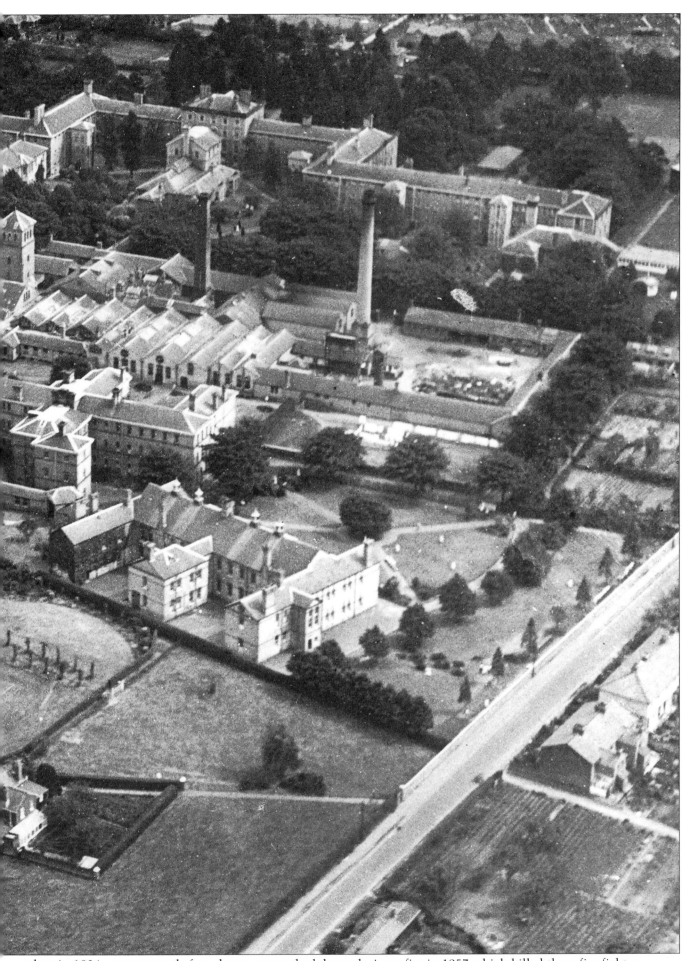

...was taken in 1934, many years before the tower crashed down during a fire in 1957 which killed three fire fighters.

Linton Hospital in 1964. It was originally a Maidstone workhouse.

The original Maidstone Grammar School in Tonbridge Road, later Maidstone Technical School for Boys.

The Grammar School for Boys relocated to Barton Road in 1930.

Maidstone Technical High School for Boys – one of many that later underwent name changes – moved to its new home at Oakwood Park, Tonbridge Road, in 1959.

Senacre Secondary School in Sutton Road in 1965, eight years after it opened.

West Borough School, like so many, was opened in the early years of the 20th century.

Not all the children at Hunton village school look pleased as their teacher stages a canteen display in 1934.

Miss D.Pritchard with her chemistry class at Maidstone Girls' Grammar School in 1949.

Happy memories – an Aylesford School concert in April 1952.

Most of the public houses, hotels and restaurants in the next sequence have long closed, been renamed or altered beyond recognition. These pictures, predominantly from the 1930s, 1940s and 1950s, remind us that they used to be as much a part of the unchanging scene as churches.

The Red Lion at the junction of High Street and Week Street, always known as the Gin Palace.

The Fortune of War in
Old Tovil Road.

The West Kent Hotel in
Week Street.

The Queen's Head Hotel in High Street.

The Nags Head in Week Street with modest Christmas decorations.

The Foresters Arms in 1936. Four years later it was destroyed by a German bomb.

The Mitre in Market Buildings.

The Queen Anne at the junction
of Queen Anne Road and
Sittingbourne Road.

The Market House
Inn in Earl Street.

The Walnut Tree at Tonbridge Road.

Maidstone's best-known hotel, the Royal Star, which dated back to the 16th century. It made way for a shopping arcade in the 1980s.

The Bull Hotel in Gabriel's Hill.

The Rose and Crown Hotel in High Street.

The Victoria Hotel in
Week Street.

The Swan in
Loose Road.

The Wheatsheaf in Loose Road.

The Blue Door in Sutton Road.

The Chiltern Hundreds in Sittingbourne Road.

The Running Horse in Sandling Road.

The New Inn near County Hall – later the Wig and Gown.

The Yew Tree at Boxley.

The Tudor House at Bearsted.

The Cock Inn at Detling.

The Chequers at West Farleigh.

The Bush, Blackbird and Thrush at East Peckham.

Maidstone at War

Britain declared war on Germany in September 1939 and preparations for the defence of the country began in earnest. Here curious pupils from North Borough School watch workmen dig trenches.

People from all walks of life soon joined in the effort. This is a group of Air Raid Precaution warden volunteers at a Maidstone meeting.

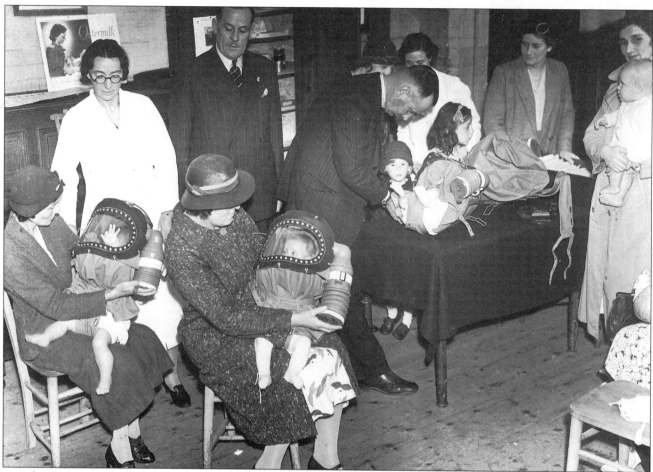

Residents of Barming are shown how to safeguard their babies with gas protectors.

This was the Local Defence Volunteer group formed at Maidstone Grammar School – hence the youth of the officer and sergeant. They were later to become part of the famous Dad's Army, the Home Guard.

The early months of the war meant that many children from the Maidstone area were evacuated from their families to safer parts of the country 'for the duration'. Ironically, Maidstone was also a reception area for evacuees from other parts of the country, like these London children arriving in 1939.

A naval officer driving this car miraculously escaped unhurt when enemy bombs landed in Mill Street one morning in October 1940.

Police lead the Mayor and Corporation of Maidstone past bomb damage in Mill Street as they made their way to a church service in November 1940.

Land girls, as they became known, helped with the harvest at Hollingbourne.

There was much talk of 'women doing men's work' during the war, never better illustrated than in the Women's Land Army. Was this the start of women's lib?

Civilians were soon getting used to queueing for almost everything. This group formed at a fishmongers in Week Street in 1941.

Lord Woolton, the Minister of Food, had warm thanks to offer members of the Women's Land Army and farm workers when he visited Allington in December 1942.

Parades and ceremonial events were held frequently to boost morale during the war. Here Admiral Sir George D'Oyly Lyon shares the Town Hall saluting base with, among others the Mayor, Alderman Sir Garrard Tyrwhitt-Drake and MP Alfred Bossom (extreme right) during Warship Week in 1942.

Surprisingly, big crowds and full ceremonial were part of the wartime scene. It's curious at this distance to see the Russian Red Flag beside the Union Jack and the Stars and Stripes for this United Nations Day gathering in the summer of 1942.

Many organisations were represented at National Call to Prayer ceremonies in September 1942. This parade was on its way to Bearsted Church.

The Governor of Nigeria, Sir Bernard Bourdillion (in the trilby), presented a mobile kitchen as a gift from the people of Nigeria, at Yalding in May 1942.

Servicewomen were looked after by volunteers at the YWCA canteen in Rose Yard, Maidstone.

Seriously-wounded servicemen came to be cared for at Preston Hall Hospital near Aylesford.

The target for Wings for Victory week in Maidstone was £1,000, a formidable sum in those days. The gung-ho feeling was obvious as youngsters at the Broadway were encouraged to stick savings stamps on a bomb 'to be dropped on Germany'.

An RAF Spitfire fighter attracted great interest in Palace Gardens as part of the Wings for Victory fund-raising in 1943.

More speech-making by the Mayor at the presentation of colours to members of the Civil Defence Corps in Lockmeadow.

Field Marshal 'Monty' Montgomery inspected troops in Mote Park in February 1944 and delivered a speech designed to lift spirits. The D-Day invasion of Europe was only a few months away.

VJ Day on 8 August 1945, heralded the return of peace for the first time in six years. Big crowds gathered for the official ceremony at Maidstone Town Hall marking the Japanese surrender.

The year 1944 brought Germany's last serious raids with the notorious flying bombs, the V1 and V2 rockets. There was nothing that could be done about the latter, but two children from this class at Otham School kept a

look-out for the V1 'doodlebugs' while the rest carried on as usual.

The rocket threat provoked further evacuation, something that war-weary parents thought had long ended. These

...oungsters were departing from Maidstone West Station.

The war in Europe ended on 8 May 1945. VE Day parties were held everywhere and the Mayoress of Maidstone, Mrs Gordon Larking, greeted a splendid 'mini version' of Prime Minister Winston Churchill at Foster Clark Estate's celebration.

Sport and Recreation

County cricket has been played at The Mote ground in Maidstone – part of Mote Park – since 1859. This was the scene in July 1931. Most of the vacant area near the ground has been extensively developed.

Despite the lack of creature comfort, the traditional Maidstone Cricket Week attracted excellent support. This scene from 1969 is a good example of spectators watching Kent in action.

Kent cricketers Colin Cowdrey (left) and Godfrey Evans were honoured at a Maidstone lunch marking their achievements in England's successful Test team in Australia during the 1954-55 winter. Between them is Lord Cornwallis, the guest speaker and a former captain and president of Kent County Cricket Club among his many distinctions.

The Mote have for long been one of Kent's leading cricket clubs. This 1965 group includes Tony Levick, the captain (seated centre), who was to serve the county club as treasurer for many years, and John Pocock (wearing pads), who later became the Kent chairman and president. Malcolm Bristow, the player standing on the right next to the umpire, had been groundsman at The Mote for 30 years when this book went to print.

The Athletic Ground in London Road, home of Maidstone United Football Club for 60 years before it was sold for development in the 1980s, a move that eventually caused the winding-up of the club. This picture was taken in pre-war days.

Maidstone United varied from professional and amateur status over the years. After suffering serious decline as a leading amateur side in the 1960s they progressed through the non-League professional ranks to become a Football League club for a short period. This action picture from the early 1970s shows the Stones at home to Faversham Town in a cup match and gives an indication of the big crowds they attracted.

Chairman Jim Thompson, the driving force behind the push to League status, with the 1971 Maidstone United squad.

Maidstone's best-known post-war footballer, David Sadler first appeared for the Stones while he was at Maidstone Technical School in 1961. He went on to play for England amateurs and then gained full international honours after signing for Manchester United. Here he celebrates his first amateur cap by pulling a pint in his father's pub, the Two Brewers, in Yalding.

Amateur football clubs have long thrived in the Maidstone area. This post-war Aylesford Paper Mills side were among the best for some years when they played in the Kent League against bigger clubs.

The Olympic torch was carried through Maidstone on its way to the 1948 Games in London.

One of Maidstone's best-ever athletes, Frank Sando, represented Britain in the 10,000 metres in the 1952 and 1956 Olympics and was in England's cross-country team for nine consecutive years. He also gained medals in the Empire and European Games. Sando, from Aylesford, was a member of Maidstone Harriers.

Enthusiastic crowds watched vehicles drive through Maidstone in the *Kent Messenger* Old Crocks Race in December 1930. The event later gave way for the more dignified veteran cars race.

Maidstone Rugby Club, officially known as Maidstone Football Club, had Arthur Marshall, president of the Rugby Union, to open their new stand at The Mote ground in 1957.

Bowls has for long been one of the most popular sports in the area. These players in 1957 enjoyed the picturesque setting of the Cobdown ground at Ditton Corner.

A formal touch to Yalding Cricket Club's game against Fremlins in 1950 as Mrs M.L.Leigh unfurls a flag and declares the new pavilion officially open.

Hill climbing was easier in a sports car. It was a sport with substantial following in the 1950s and 1960s. This Sunday scene was at Boxley.

Kart racing – then known as go-kart racing – came to Maidstone for the first time in April 1960, but proved a short-lived attraction.

Another sport that failed to catch on was trotting, although a vast crowd estimated at 10,000 turned up for this opening meeting at Kent County Showground at Detling on Easter Monday 1968.

Fox hunting had not been subjected to controversy and disruption when this meet set off from Yalding in 1968. It was simply part of the accepted rural scene.

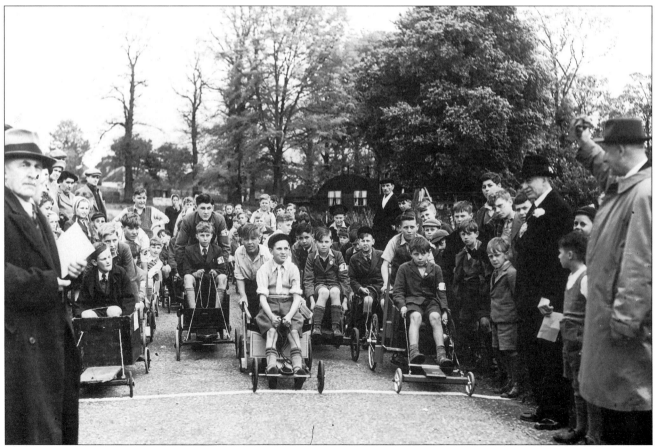

Lots of boys made soap box carts in the days when pleasures were decidedly more simple than today. This was the start of the Mote Park soap box derby in 1950, with the Mayor, Alderman W.Day, doing the honours.

Tranquillity unlimited in Maidstone's superb Mote Park in 1962. The park was purchased by the corporation from Viscount Bearsted in 1928 and opened to the public the following year. Since then it has been used for all forms of outdoor recreation.

In 1961 fairly formal dress was still the order of the day to play pitch and putt at Mote Park.

Fairs and circuses were regular features of life in Maidstone up to the 1960s. This was one of those organised

e *Kent Messenger* Keg Megs Club soon after World War Two.

The miniature railway, with its precision models, was a constant delight for young visitors to Mote Park.

Maidstone Carnival remains one of the key features of town life. This was the Sharps Kreemy mermaids float in 1937.

Mote Park was the home of the Kent County Agricultural Show until it moved to permanent headquarters at Detling in 1964. This 1962 view reveals that the show had not developed into the major commercial enterprise of today.

One of the main parades at a Mote Park County Show.

Fremlins brought its message to the show public with this appealing 1950s float.

Fine style in evidence at a coaching marathon at the 1950 show.

The ageless appeal of steam naturally attracted attention at the 1971 show at Detling.

Recreation or hard work? Champion R.Martin in action at the Weald of Kent ploughing match at Linton in the 1950s.

The Surrounding Area

Leeds Castle in the 1940s when it was in the hands of its last private owner, Lady Baillie. Originally built in the ninth century and later a royal residence, Leeds Castle was in recent years to become a highly-successful commercial enterprise promoted as 'the loveliest castle in the world'.

Allington Castle in 1955. Built in the reign of Edward I, it later became home to Sir Thomas Wyatt the elder and his son, who led the unsuccessful Kentish Rebellion of 1554.

Carmelite nuns at their
Allington Castle retreat
in 1958.

The civic opening of
Allington Lock in 1937.

The Medway in the Allington area has long been favoured for boating and fishing. This picture of complete calm was taken in 1956.

Lord Cornwallis tests his skill at the ancient quintain at Offham. This was during a celebration in 1945 to mark the restoration of the quintain, used in previous centuries by knights practising for jousts. It is now the only remaining example of its kind in England.

A 1950s view of Sutton Valance School, which overlooks the area where the Weald of Kent begins.

Trottiscliffe – known as Trosley – in the 1950s. People don't walk in the middle of village streets today.

Linton Hill in the mid-1960s.

An outstanding Kent landmark, Linton Park can be seen a long way off as it is approached from the Weald.

Lord Cornwallis and his son, Capt the Hon Stanley Cornwallis, at the final meet of Linton Beagles at Linton Park House in 1932. Capt Cornwallis, later also Lord Cornwallis, was a distinguished soldier, local authority leader and sportsman and served for many years as Lord Lieutenant of Kent.

Remembrance Day at Yalding, 11 November 1965.

'A woman's place...' This was East Malling in the 1950s.

East Malling Research Station, which specialised in agricultural work, in the 1950s.

Youngsters fishing for tiddlers at Ditton pond in 1952.

A charming view of the Medway Valley in 1954 – boys at play still wore jackets and ties.

One of the most-pictured scenes in the Maidstone area – cricket at Bearsted Green in 1939.

Boxley given an artistic treatment in 1970.

Blessing the crops at Rogation Sunday service at Boxley in the 1950s.

Barming was the end of one of the Maidstone trolley bus service lines for many years until closure in 1967, three years after this picture was taken.

East Farleigh locks were rebuilt in 1938.

It could be almost anywhere in Kent at almost any time – this was actually East Farleigh in 1957.

Aylesford in 1952, when drivers were already struggling to cope with the problems of a 14th-century bridge.

Carmelite Friars in procession at Aylesford in the early 1950s.

Aylesford Priory was destroyed by fire in 1931. The Friars returned after its rebuilding in 1949.

The Roman Catholic Bishop of Southwark celebrated high mass at Aylesford Priory in 1959 with 6,000 children and teachers at the annual pilgrimage.

A 1951 picture of the famous Kits Coty Stones near Aylesford. They are reputed to mark the grave of a local leader slain in battle by Saxons in the fifth century.

Reed's paper mills at Tovil in 1963. The chimneys were demolished in the 1980s.

An untidy-looking Tovil in the 1950s.

Cars had to give way to cattle at milking time in Hollingbourne in this 1950s scene.

The Great Danes hotel at Hollingbourne in 1962 before it was extensively developed.

The Queen of Tonga went to All Saints' Church at Hollingbourne during her visit to Britain for the 1953 coronation celebrations.

A Remembrance Day service at the Cross cut in the hills near Lenham, in 1930.

A 1950s picture of one of the pageants which were a feature of life in Lenham.

Teston – pronounced Teeson – in 1953, with Barham Court in the background. The mediaeval bridge survives, but steam trains have long gone.

A 1963 picture of fishing and boating at Teston locks.

Marden in the autumn of 1963.

Sea Cadets honour the memory of Rear Admiral Charles Davis, the first man to win the Victoria Cross in 1854, at a ceremony in Mereworth Churchyard in 1956.

A 1959 fashion show at Mereworth Castle in aid of charity.

The end of this batsman's stay at the wicket in Nettlestead in 1963.

The Medway at Yalding – peaceful enough in this 1955 scene – has unfortunately seen several drowning tragedies over the years.

Frittenden in 1966 with the inn sign of the John Jorrocks prominent.

Loose stream – a glorious 1965 picture.

Loose in the snows of 1970, as beautiful as ever.

West Malling in 1947.

Subscribers

R C & M Adams
Mrs D Alexander
J F Ashbee
Kathleen Ashley

Enid Bartter
Joan Beddous
Geraldine Benjamin
Roger Bettle
Clive Birchall
Mr A Bray
Brian Brenchley
Roy S Brooker
D F Buffery
Robert James Burr
Mary Busbridge
Mr C A Butcher
J J Butcher

Brian Cannell
Mr W J Carden
Patricia A Castle
Matthew & Ian Chinn
Lawrence Allix Cleggett
Sheila E Collins
Jane Cork

Mrs M J Davis
Patricia A Drury

Alan S Edridge
Maurice Gordon Emery

David Field
Frank Ford

Malcolm V Gladwin
Mr K M J Golding
Mr Raymond Douglas Gravenell
Mr & Mrs Robert Greengrow

Mrs Joyce Hales
Alan & Joyce Hales
Angela & Barrie Harber
Mr Harry Forrester

G Hardwell
Mr Paul Hollands
Mrs Mabel Hosking
Stanley N Hughes
John Hunt

Sheila M Iles

Alan Larcombe
Maxine Love
Linda C Lucas

Ann McNae
Adam & Greg McPherson
Ronald Mabb
Maidstone Priority Care NHS Trust
Daphne Margerum
Angela Martin
James William Martin
Mr N P Matthews
Darren Mark May
Leslie Thomas May
Tina Linda May
Mr A Maynard
R E C Moore
Mrs Heather Morris
Jason Munn

Brian Nolan

Trevor Owens

Linda Parker
B G Pateman
David Penny

John Frederick Philpott
Joyce Pilcher
Mrs M A Pipe
Mrs Carol A Pryce
Raymond D Pyman

Leonard Reeves
Mark & Sue Reumel
Peter Reynolds

Gordon Samson
Frances M Smith
Janet Jacqueline Smith
James R Smith
Peter Smith
Norman B Spary
Mrs P L Strawgroom

Mr & Mrs A Styles
D R Taylor
G W Taylor
Eileen M Terry
Joan Tong
Leslie A Trafford
Mr C Tutt

Malcolm F Walkinshaw
Mr F P Wallond
Ida White
Ken White
Roy F Wicken
Richard A Wood
N E Wright